Book 3

G

The Graded Piano Player

Well-known tunes specially arranged by leading educationalists

FABER *ff* MUSIC

© 2016 by Faber Music Ltd
Bloomsbury House
74–77 Great Russell Street
London
WC1B 3DA

Music setting by MusicSet2000
Cover design by Chloë Alexander
Page design by Susan Clarke

Printed in England by Caligraving Ltd

ISBN10: 0-571-53942-4
EAN13: 978-0-571-53942-0

To buy Faber Music publications or to find out about the full range of titles available
please contact your local music retailer or Faber Music sales enquiries:
Faber Music Ltd, Burnt Mill, Elizabeth Way, Harlow CM20 2HX
Tel: +44 (0) 1279 82 89 82   Fax: 44 (0) 1279 82 89 83
sales@fabermusic.com   fabermusicstore.com

Contents

Consider yourself

from *Oliver*

Arranged by Christopher Hussey

Words and Music by Lionel Bart

With a bounce

Feeling good

Arranged by Ned Bennett

Words and Music by Leslie Bricusse
and Anthony Newley

Shenandoah

Arranged by Ned Bennett

Traditional

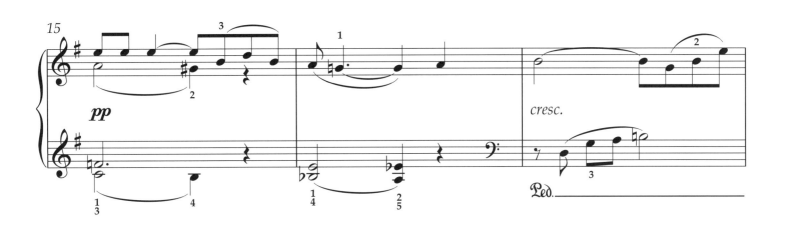

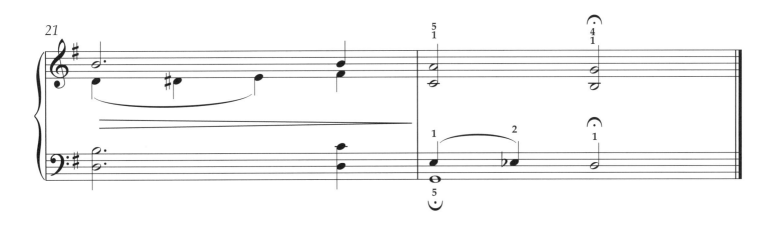

If I ruled the world

Arranged by Christopher Hussey

Words by Leslie Bricusse
Music by Cyril Ornadel

Bonny at morn

Arranged by Ned Bennett

Traditional

Circle of life

from Walt Disney Pictures' *The Lion King*

Arranged by Ned Bennett

Music by Elton John
Lyrics by Tim Rice

15

Goldfinger

Arranged by Ned Bennett

Music by John Barry
Lyrics by Anthony Newley and Leslie Bricusse

He's a pirate

from Walt Disney Pictures' *Pirates of the Caribbean: The Curse of the Black Pearl*

Klaus Badelt

(They long to be) Close to you

Arranged by Ned Bennett

Words by Hal David
Music by Burt Bacharach

If I were a rich man

from *Fiddler on the roof*

Arranged by Alan Bullard

Words by Sheldon Harnick
Music by Jerry Bock

Doctor Who

Ron Grainer

Driving swing tempo

Let it go

from Disney's Animated Feature *Frozen*

Arranged by Alan Bullard

Music and Lyrics by Kristen Anderson-Lopez and Robert Lopez

Cry me a river

Arranged by Ned Bennett

Words and Music by Arthur Hamilton

Pride and prejudice

Carl Davis

Allegro ma non troppo

Wayfaring stranger

Arranged by Alan Bullard

Traditional